Fantastic Cats

Scottish Fold

Sierra Wilson

AV2
www.openlightbox.com

Fantastic Cats

Scottish Fold

Contents

Name the Cat

Which cat has ears that fold on top of its head?

Which cat likes to sit up like a prairie dog?

Which cat is social and does not like to be alone?

The Scottish Fold Cat!

Meet the Scottish Fold

Pet owners looking for a unique cat with a lovable personality might want to consider the Scottish fold **breed**. Scottish folds have a distinct look, with big eyes and ears held close to their round heads. However, many Scottish folds can experience health issues due to their **genetics**.

Despite their known health issues, Scottish folds are **low-maintenance** cats. This trait, along with their sweet **dispositions**, make the Scottish fold a favorite among many people. Celebrity owners and well-known cats have also contributed to a recent increase in the breed's popularity.

The Scottish Fold Breed

Scottish fold **ears** can be **single**, **double**, or **triple** folded.

About **50 percent** of Scottish folds have folded ears. Those with straight ears are known as **Scottish straights**.

With proper care, healthy Scottish folds can live for up to **15 years**.

Scottish Fold History

In 1961, British shepherd William Ross noticed that Susie, a barn cat in his neighborhood, had folded ears. He adopted one of Susie's kittens and began developing a new breed. By 1966, Ross's Scottish fold cats were registered with the Governing Council of the Cat Fancy (GCCF), a cat **pedigree registry** in the United Kingdom.

The same **genetic mutation** that causes these cats' ears to fold may also cause them to experience some painful health conditions. The GCCF stopped registering Scottish folds in the 1970s due to these health concerns. Some countries, such as Austria, have even banned the breeding of these cats. However, the breed's popularity continued to grow in the United States and other parts of the world. A substantial contribution to Scottish fold fame comes from renowned owners and cats on social media. For instance, American singer Taylor Swift has two Scottish fold cats. British singer Ed Sheeran's Scottish fold and domestic shorthair cats have more than 250,000 followers on Instagram.

Japan

Japan is home to one of the best-known Scottish folds in the world. In 2021, Scottish fold Motimaru set a Guinness World Record. His videos on YouTube were watched more than 600 million times, making him the most viewed cat on the platform. His record was broken in 2022, but Motimaru's channel still has about 2 million subscribers today.

Folded Ears and Big Eyes

When Scottish fold kittens are born, their ears are straight. Then, after 3 to 4 weeks, some of the kittens' ears begin to fold over. These Scottish folds are prized both as pets and as show cats.

EYES
The big, round eyes of Scottish folds come in different colors, including blue, copper, gold, green, and blue-green.

FUR
Scottish fold fur can be either long or short. It comes in a wide variety of colors and patterns.

HEAD

The head of a Scottish fold looks particularly round. Some people say that this head, together with the folded ears, makes Scottish folds look like owls.

BODY

Scottish folds are medium-sized cats. They are sturdy and have soft, padded bodies that appear rounded.

EARS

Their unique ears are the best-known characteristic of Scottish folds. The ears fold down and forward against the head, making it look like the cat is wearing a little bonnet.

Sweet Personalities

Scottish folds are easy to get along with. They have sweet, gentle personalities and do well with children and other pets. Scottish folds are social and do not like being left alone for long periods of time. For this reason, pairing one with a companion cat can be useful. These cats also enjoy being around their family. Although they are not demanding, they are **affectionate** and will follow their owners from room to room. They are happy to enjoy cuddles and lap time. Scottish folds also like to play.

Scottish folds are **adaptable** cats that can thrive in many different home environments. They are intelligent and curious. These cats have a few different behaviors that many owners find **endearing**. For example, some Scottish folds sit up on their rear legs like prairie dogs when they hear an interesting sound.

Happy and Playful

Scottish folds enjoy being playful. They may learn tricks, such as opening cabinets or playing fetch. Scottish folds especially enjoy toys they can chase. Rotating toys on a weekly basis helps keep these cats interested in playing with them. Finding treats hidden around the house is another fun game for Scottish folds. Owners should spend time playing with their Scottish folds every day to form a stronger bond with them. This also keeps the cats active, helping them maintain a healthy weight.

Scottish folds have medium energy and activity levels. This means that they thrive on a mix of active play and calm cuddle time. Some Scottish folds have sensitive or stiff tails. When playing with or petting a Scottish fold, people should be careful to handle the tail very gently to avoid causing pain.

Make a Cat Wand

Engaging toys are a must for intelligent cats such as Scottish folds. Many interesting toys can be purchased in stores. Others can be made at home using common objects.

One simple, easy-to-make cat toy is a cat wand. Only ordinary items, such as a stick, a fork, yarn, and a pair of scissors, are needed to make this toy. First, create pom-poms. To do so. wrap the yarn around the fork's **tines** and tie a knot around the wrapped yarn. Then, slide the yarn off the fork. With the help of an adult, cut the yarn on both sides of the knot to obtain a pom-pom. After enough pom-poms have been created, the remaining yarn can be used to create a braid. Attach the pom-poms to the braid. Finally, attach the braid to the stick. The cat wand can be used to provide your cat with healthy **stimulation** and entertainment.

Caring for Your Scottish Fold

Overall, Scottish folds are easy to care for. One special need they have is related to their ears. Pet owners should check their Scottish fold's ears weekly and clean them with cat ear cleaner and a cotton ball or small towel, if needed. Checking their cat's ears regularly also helps owners spot any signs of irritation or infection.

Scottish folds have dense fur that should be brushed weekly. Luckily, these cats often enjoy being brushed as a form of play. Along with caring for Scottish fold ears and fur, trimming their claws every couple of weeks and making time for active play will help keep these cats in great shape.

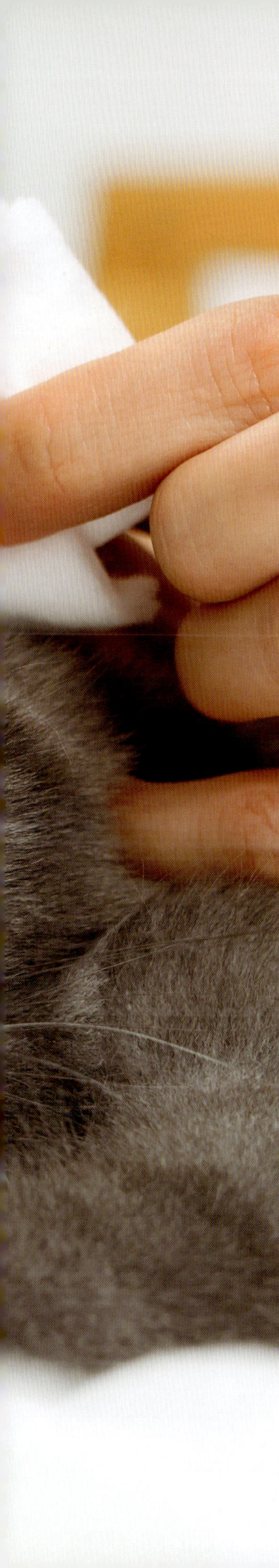

Cat Supplies

Ear Cleaner A mix of water and cider vinegar can be used to clean a Scottish fold's ears. Special cat ear cleaning products can also be recommended by a **veterinarian**.

Litter Box To avoid a mess, Scottish folds need a litter box that is cleaned regularly. Sometimes, owners may need to purchase several litter boxes before finding one their cat will use.

Scratching Post Like other cats, Scottish folds have a scratching **instinct**. A scratching post gives cats an appropriate place to scratch and can help protect furniture.

Steel Comb A steel comb or cat brush should be used to brush a Scottish fold's fur. Brushing or combing helps avoid **hairballs** and matted fur, keeping Scottish folds looking their best.

Healthy Scottish Folds

Like all cats, Scottish folds should see a veterinarian regularly and receive routine **vaccinations**. A veterinarian can check for health problems and give advice on proper cat care. Scottish folds should also have their teeth brushed daily, be fed a healthy diet, and be given plenty of fresh, clean water.

Scottish folds have specific health challenges. One of the biggest health concerns for these cats is a serious condition called osteochondrodysplasia. This condition causes bone and **cartilage** problems that lead to stiffness and pain. Some Scottish folds with this condition have trouble walking and moving normally. To reduce the chances of health issues, pet owners should carefully select a kitten from a responsible **breeder**.

Average Weight of Pet Cats

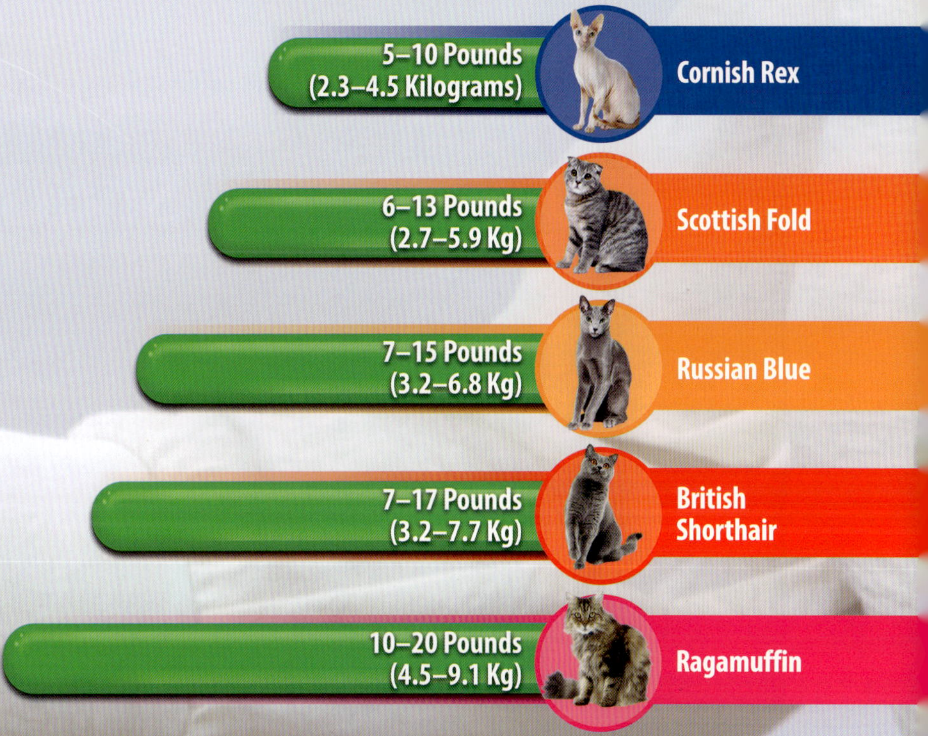

If You Like Scottish Fold Cats...

Some cats resemble Scottish folds in appearance. Others share a similar disposition. If you like Scottish folds, here are some other cat breeds you might enjoy.

American Curl

American curls share their curled ears with the Scottish fold. Breeders started developing the American curl breed in the 1980s. These cats are affectionate with people and good with other pets. Some people call them "the Peter Pan of cats" for their kitten-like personality.

British Shorthair

British shorthairs have dense fur and round eyes. They are affectionate and easygoing. These cats generally have good health. Scottish folds are often bred with British shorthairs to help breeders raise healthy kittens with folded ears.

Exotic Shorthair

Much like Scottish folds, exotic shorthairs have large, round eyes and a charming appearance. This breed was created by breeding American shorthairs with Persian cats. Exotic shorthairs are calm but playful and like to be with their family. They can do well with both children and other animals.

Ragdoll

Like Scottish folds, Ragdolls have sweet personalities and make good family pets. They are among the largest cats and can reach weights of 20 pounds (9.1 kg). Their name comes from they way they go floppy, like rag dolls, when they are being held.

Russian Blue

Russian blues are loving and intelligent. Like Scottish folds, they are fairly easy to care for. They like to be near their family but can be shy around strangers. Russian blues are known for their thick, soft, gray-blue fur.

Scottish Fold Quiz

1 What percentage of Scottish folds have folded ears?

2 Who first developed the Scottish fold breed?

3 Which colors can a Scottish fold's eyes be?

4 How long can healthy Scottish fold cats live?

5 What is the average weight of a Scottish fold cat?

6 Which cat breed is often bred with Scottish folds?

7 Which body part of some Scottish folds is stiff and sensitive?

8 What is a Scottish straight?

Answers:
1. About 50 percent **2.** William Ross
3. Blue, copper, gold, green, and blue-green **4.** Up to 15 years
5. 6 to 13 pounds (2.7 to 5.9 kg)
6. British shorthair **7.** The tail
8. A Scottish fold that does not develop the folded ears

Key Words

adaptable: someone or something that can easily adjust to new conditions
affectionate: loving or caring
breed: a group of animals with similar characteristics and family history
breeder: a person who raises and sells young animals
cartilage: firm, flexible tissue in the body
dispositions: personalities
endearing: inspiring love
genetic mutation: an inherited change that affects the cells of living beings and causes unusual physical characteristics
genetics: the information, contained inside the cells of the body, that determines the physical features of a living being
hairballs: balls of hair that may form inside a cat's stomach
instinct: a natural behavior with which animals are born
low-maintenance: easy to care for
pedigree registry: an organization in charge of certifying that individual animals belong to a specific breed
stimulation: encouragement to become active
tines: the prongs of a fork
vaccinations: medical treatments that produce immunity against specific diseases
veterinarian: a doctor for animals

Index

Published by Lightbox Learning Inc.
276 5th Avenue
Suite 704 #917
New York, NY 10001
Website: www.openlightbox.com

Library of Congress Cataloging-in-Publication Data available upon request

ISBN 978-1-7911-5618-3 (hardcover)
ISBN 978-1-7911-5619-0 (softcover)
ISBN 978-1-7911-5620-6 (multi-user eBook)

Printed in Guangzhou, China
1 2 3 4 5 6 7 8 9 0 27 26 25 24 23

042023
101122

Project Coordinator: Sara Cucini
Designer: Terry Paulhus
Layout: Jean Faye Marie Rodriguez

Photo Credits
Every reasonable effort has been made to trace ownership and to obtain permission to reprint copyright material. The publisher would be pleased to have any errors or omissions brought to its attention so that they may be corrected in subsequent printings. The publisher acknowledges Alamy, Getty Images, and Shutterstock as its primary image suppliers for this title.